KATE KELLY

BARKING AT SUNSPOTS

& other poems

Drawings & Paintings By Nancy Olivier

Some of these poems have appeared in *DICO, Voices International, Oasis D'Neon* and *AITIA Magazine,* and in the 1987 edition of *The American Poetry Anthology.*

BARKING AT SUNSPOTS

First Edition, 1987

ISBN 0-918537-01-0

Library of Congress Catalog Card Number
86-83047

JUSTIN BOOKS
41 Greenwich Ave.
New York, NY 10014

Manufactured in the United States of America

BARKING AT SUNSPOTS
and other poems

In the eyes of men he falls, and in his own eyes too. He falls from his high place, he trips on his achievement. He falls to you, he falls to know you. It is sad, they say. See his disgrace, say the ones at his heel. But he falls radiantly toward the light to which he falls. They cannot see who lifts him as he falls, or how his falling changes, and he himself bewildered till his heart cries out to bless the one who holds him in his falling. And in his fall he hears his heart cry out, his heart explains why he is falling, why he had to fall, and he gives over to the fall. Blessed are you, clasp of the falling. He falls into the sky, he falls into the light, none can hurt him as he falls. Blessed are you, shield of the falling. Wrapped in his fall, concealed within his fall, he finds the place, he is gathered in. While his hair streams back and his clothes tear in the wind, he is held up, comforted, he enters into the place of his fall. Blessed are you, embrace of the falling, foundation of the light, master of the human accident. — Leonard Cohen

FOR MY TEACHER

TABLE OF CONTENTS

*Available On Cassette
 Send $8. Check or Money Order to:
 JUSTIN BOOKS
 41 Greenwich Ave.
 N.Y., N.Y. 10014

Nancy Olivier is a painter living in New York City

Reproductions of original paintings and drawings
by Nancy Olivier appear on the following pages:

19, 30, 34, 45, 47, 57, 61, 68, 71, 73, 77, 86, 89, 93,
96, 101, 114, 117, 122, 133, 137.

Cover design by Nancy Olivier.

MONKEY SEE, MONKEY DO

I stole the rope from the bottom of your soles
and strung up a bulb in front of your eyes
and watched the colors turn to mud.
I pulled out a tube of blue and thinned it
with blood from my finger and commenced
an experiment of awesome dimension.
The bulb burst from the heat.
I felt my way in the dark
with the ease of a person born blind
at birth.
You licked your lips and I laughed
at your spittle.
I tugged at your ears and your
tongue shot out.
I tickled the nape of your neck and
you tap danced left and right and
rewarded me with a soft cry of surprise.
I sewed a tail between your legs and
clipped your nails and spun the hairs
on your head.
Now, I said, *we are ready for the ark.*

THE LAST TIME I WAS IN FRANCE

I located Van Gogh's house in Arles
and in the Van Gogh Tavern
I drank pernod.
The streets were cobblestone and
crowded with bicycles and
those peasant stock ladies
with their peculiar charm.

I lost myself in a department
store and in the record section
I bought the song that was playing.
I didn't know the words
but the voice
was very beautiful.

I kept asking where my three
friends were but I found
out later I'd mixed up the language
and was in fact
asking where my three countrysides
were.

The last time I was in France
it is no wonder
that all the ladies and even the
bicycles looked at me as if
I were a
crazy
American.

AN ITCH TO LIVE

Behind this mask of rouge
and melting grease paint
my features freeze
            like icy pipes
till hot cigar smoke
            wraps around my fear
like a comfortable dirty cloak.

When I go under
I trust blind chance
            like faith
to fish me out
and catch my flesh
            with dog teeth.

Like a cat
            sitting at a window
I scratch at the screen
for life outside
and itch to live
            within
the screaming distance of a city.

A NIGHT WITH THE GYPSIES

I was never afraid of the sun.
I always treasured the hotness and wetness,
they were as invaluable as jewels.
And so, when I was summoned to darkness and
its full-lipped secret entrance into madness,
it is fair to say
I feared for my virtue.
I sought to hide under a rock
but encountered there
snakes of every description, each with
a ravenous appetite for my flawless pulse.
I stole away quickly, panicked by
the hellish sound that defiled the sun's
stunning silence.
Still the darkness ate at my heels, and
finally it, quite like a net, surrounded me
on all sides.
A voice whispered, "are you cold?"
I answered, "I'll live."
It was not for me a question of pride.
It was a test of endurance.
But privately I was freezing as the night wind
stole away the heat that engages my trust.

In the blackness I sensed a mad mesh
of bloody politics and heady cabaret.
Then, two screams sounded, one
from a pair of wild eyes, a second
from the tips of painted fingernails.
A voice whispered in my ear,
"It is so effective to do the unimaginable,
though difficult to master, no?"
With my nun's hands, quite unpracticed in
darkness, I knelt and prayed.
Suddenly the music grew louder.

Someone dressed in a tunisian cape
held a live chicken by its neck.
I prayed faster. They were summoning the devil.
My hands trembled.

"Do not fear," a voice whispered,
"we summon the devil only to catch it and
free the people from its deathgrip. It has
been our purpose for a thousand years
to revisit the lands of our ancient migrations.
We are outcasts in every society and
only the rhythm of our sorrow
allows us to survive. Wait and see.
Later we will summon the Black Madonna.
You see, all our fingers are at work.
You see our spiralling hands?
Travel with us the pilgrim's trail.
Let us be heard!"

In one quick motion a knife severed
the head off the chicken.
I could not watch.

"The head,
the head is the tip of the iceberg
staring down ships in the night,
glinting in the sun's light, a
persistent melting eye of the storm."

The words were chanted at a fast and furious clip
against a tapestry of flamenco music.
A thousand voices repeated,

"The head,
the head is the tip of the iceberg
staring down ships in the night,
glinting in the sun's light, a
persistent melting eye of the storm."

My face felt hot.
It was wet and sticky. It was covered with
the blood of a chicken.
I screamed and all fell silent.
The blackness was like a hole and I
at its center, wept soundlessly.
The same voice as before broke the silence.
"You are a daughter of the sun.
You should not weep. The sun rises in the East.
The East is mysterious, sandalfooted. It
tip toes through seasons and centuries
biding time, illumed by the flame eternal.
Well, go back then, if you must,
go back to your light and sun.
But remember the *duende,* the spirit of
darkness, will one day be heard and you must
prepare yourself for its secret music.
Return to the sun child, with one thought,
If there is no God
It must be the Devil laughing at mankind."

I awakened, embraced by the sun's strength.
I ran to a pool of water and sought in it the
reflection of my face.
It was unchanged save a sinful stain of red
around my eyes.
I fell to my knees to thank God my virtue
was still intact,
but my hands could not find each other.
I laughed soundlessly.

LETTER TO A YOUNG ARTIST

To win the confidence of the poor
You must say what you see, touch what you love
And know what you will lose.
The image of your dream, and the
Object of your memory
Are each one half of your destiny.

Your infinite loneliness will gestate into
A great solitude to work in.
Give birth to your art, and
Send it out to a hostile world,
A messenger of love and its
Greatest commandments:

To live without fear of death.
To dream without fear of waking.
To hold dear the innocence of the sexes.
To practice charity.
To force the omen of crisis to its knees.
To beg a flower live forever unmolested.
To trace lovingly the outline of hate
And wrench from the heart of living things
Purity.
To embrace the seamy side of life and
Encourage the union of every lovely
Imagination.
To save the planet for our children's children.
To engage the mind, the heart and
The hand in debate.
To summon forth from every confusion
One clear moment.

To win the confidence of the poor
You must say what you see, touch what you love
And know what you will lose.

WHEN YOUR SHADOW IS ENORMOUS

When
    your shadow is enormous
        the sun can't find itself
    suddenly it's all darkness
        and even the constellations
        weep.

When
    your shadow looms
        the earth is made small and
    suddenly it's a stones throw
        to
        hell.

Well
    would you please sit down?
        It's springtime
    and the flowers
        are
        miserable.

BARKING AT SUNSPOTS

I'm snapped at the stem, pruned
like a bonsai;
sunspots dance a tango in my eye.
Who's gonna thread me through this jungle
and return the radio to my car?
Papa?

Papa reminds me I lost my dog
a thousand years ago
when a tidal wave ran over my
fingerprints. Hey! What's
a leash but a handy line to drop
in bad company?

I got a monkey on my back, pop.
It's clever and manipulative.
It curls its tail around the sky
when I count the planes that
cross over my roof at night.
Then I run out of fingers.

One of these nights I'm gonna
witness a catastrophe. "But until then,"
Mama mocks, "who's lookin' at you?"
"And who's bleedin' who?" I ask.
Our eyes don't connect but
our heartbeats flip.

I work my bones to the finger to
hone a stunning attitude of
indifference. I call heads *and* tails.
The coin lands on its edge
and rolls off into the sunset
like Gary Cooper in *High Noon*.

It's high time that white lies
made their mark on this lily white soul
of mine
and announce a thousands shades of grey.
I can no longer define the difference
between trapping mice and murder one.

The bugs in my apartment are angry.
They had to climb four flights of stairs,
In my phantom voice I echo their pain,
"The beauty of my wings deceived me!"
I hear raw laughter
in the wings off-stage.

I display my collection of
5,000 empty books of matches
and draw a crowd.
A conceptualist's tail is always
on fire and
chasing itself.

Edgar A. Poe visited my rooms and the
ceiling and walls started closing in.
I drew in my breath through flared
nostrils and
fell through a tunnel
like Alice did.

Mine was a flawless performance.
My ears flattened back.
A light beckoned but my monkey sense
told me to flutter my eyelids
and twitch the third finger
on my left hand.

My puny chest rose and cut a naked path
through the sharp excitement

in the air.
I exhaled and inhaled and exhaled and
at last I heard the peculiar laughter
of a defrocked priest.

Mama strokes my sixth sense and papa
calls me the way you call a dog to dinner.
I returned whole from an unpopular war
but on Fridays in August I bark at the moon
and on occasion
I roll over and play dead.

A CHEAP SLEEP AT THE CHELSEA HOTEL

On the other side
of this cheap hotel wall
the very thick lipped groan of lust
is audible.
Perhaps it truly is love.

This wall is so thin.
I can't resist the temptation
to press my ear against it.
I am unashamed.
Perhaps it truly is love.

The soft moans are the clear clean sound
of pleasure found in stained sheets
and practiced flesh; opening and
closing, rhythmic and so
apparently passionate.

My jealousy is unbounded.
My suspicions well founded.
I am the uninvited guest
crashing a party for two.
Perhaps it truly is love.

My ear is burning as is
the place between my thighs.
Even my eyes are wet.
This is truly the greatness to be found
in cheap hotels.

One is never alone. One is always wet.
One anticipates the wall's defect.
Finally it is noiseless.
Exhausted, I sleep soundly
and dream of infant fingers.

CRISIS

Crisis
when you listen for your heart
beat but all that answers your ear
is the mechanical hum of something
you can't get next to
crisis
when your unfed desires rage inside
your head, deregulate your mind,
hunger and burn in your palms
upturned
crisis
when your eye in the mirror returns
the stare of cracked egg white and
yellow, mocking definition, lacking
synergy
crisis
when your limbs are leaden, weighted,
unwilling, slack and flapping
like the wings on a stuffed bird
rotting
crisis
when the muscles in your tongue, ones
you never knew you had, fail your instinct
to scream bloody
murder
crisis
when your sacred room metamorphoses into
a box-like thing with four sides,
top and bottom sealed
tight
crisis
when you reach, in your dream, the place
where all hands cross out time, and all
the hours of laughter disappear in an
instant
crisis

when the soles of your shoes melt into
the tar on the roof, and you find yourself
poised forever on the
edge
crisis
when your belly fattens, not with life but
liquor, and your veins swell on your wrist
begging a
slice
crisis
when your second half addresses you with
the formal announcement of the
intention to
defect
crisis
when your fingernails talk back at you
without kindness or beauty, and your scars,
that were your identity, fade like an
hysterical pregnancy
crisis
when the words you treasure like jewels
fail you, and the smell of paint snares you
and the laces on your boots hang like
nooses
crisis
when the plants you tend fold up for good
because your window is sunless and the water
is as impure as the pictures hanging on your
wall
crisis
when the mole on your shoulder assumes
a dark color and irregular border, and
you empty a bottle of aspirin and a quart of
vodka
crisis
when you jump up to answer the phone and
the receiver is dead and then a
devil whispers in your ear,
"Hey, what's keepin' you?"

THE CHAIN LETTER

48 hours ago I received a chain letter in the mail. This never happened to me before and I was excited to have received such important mail. But I'm afraid nothing is very simple in my life and this has complicated it further. The letter warned me that if I didn't send out twenty copies of the letter within the next 96 hours something awful would happen to me. Now it is already 48 hours later and I'm still wrestling with the idea of whether or not to follow the instructions and heed the warning or challenge fate and refuse to dwell on the dire consequences that might befall me. The letter described the incredible good luck that was rewarded those who followed the instructions. One man won a million dollars three days after he mailed out the letter to twenty people. On the other hand, a woman who threw the letter into the garbage, lost her husband the next day. What good fortune, I thought, to have won a million dollars! What rotten luck to lose a husband. But did either of these occurences have anything at all to do with this piece of paper that stares back at me? My instincts rise against such folly but somewhere in the back of my head I sense a hint of danger that discourages a hasty decision. It is my misfortune that I always have trouble with orders of any kind. I often challenge authority to prove my independence. But just now my father is in the hospital to undergo a simple operation that is described as routine and uncomplicated. Even he said not to make the trip to visit him as he would be back at home with my mother in a matter of days. All of a sudden his operation is no longer routine and is now decidedly complex and worrisome. I am holding the scalpel. I am administering the anasthesia. I am a nurse injecting the wrong medication and I am a blundering doctor

who cuts off a leg by mistake. I hold his life in my hands and it is this letter in my hands that is his life in my hands and my hands tremble. I think of every argument I ever had with my father and I think too of our sweet reconciliations. I see his eyes closing. I see the great hulk of his body under the sheet and his belly opening under the knife. I smell the sweet scent of flowers mingling with the stench of unhealed wounds. My hands are the color of fresh blood. The clock is ticking loudly and everything in me rises against this attack on my sensibilities. Who knows that I have received this letter except the person who sent it to me? That person was just following orders. That person is not responsible. I am just one of twenty people. How can it have anything at all to do with my father? I have 48 hours more to wonder.

NOTHING HAPPENED

No,
no, nothing happened to speak of
so
I don't speak of it
and that is why
there is no justice.

Hundreds of times I've been to the sun
and didn't tell anyone
because
who would believe
how I paled before her majesty?

If everything is upside down
it's too late to say anything.
Between struggling to right things
and find my tongue too,
I am alternately
a spider and its web.

MY MASTER SONG

My Master's beauty is a thorn.
My Master's eyes are an army.
A lock of My Master's hair
is a rope and hangs me.
My Master makes me kneel
a thousand feet.
My Master's body escapes
the hunter.
My Master's arms are beautiful.
My Master is endurance.
My Master is censored.
My Master is a fallen sparrow.
My Master testifies against me.
My Master's bones are gold.
My Master dances the rhumba.
My Master is shepherd and assassin.
My Master is in ruin.

My Master is a wild garden and
a castle. My Master is violating
the skin on my drum.
My Master is pilgrim.
My Master is a flock of ravens.
My Master is an archer, a counsellor,
and a snake.
My Master is law.
My Master is love and hate.
My Master is a childless kite.
My Master is drowning in the water.
My Master is landed.
My Master is a chimney and smoking,
is a jester joking.

My Master is an angel and I
wrestle My Master underneath the table.

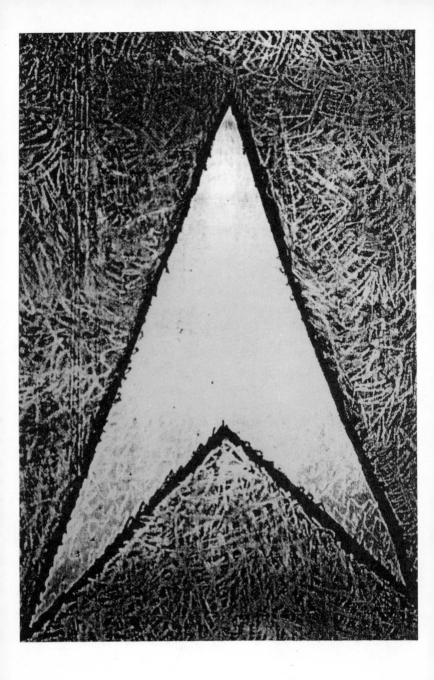

My Master is the empty road,
my journal.
My Master is parable and ark.
My Master is a spark of sky.
My Master is alibi.
My Master conspires and inspires,
confides in and sides with thieves.
My Master is an opium den, a
transistor radio.
My Master is a suicide, a cancer,
an ambition and a prohibition.
My Master is slave and slave owner,
a long sentence and a comma.

My Master is a soft black sky.

My Master's thorn is a beauty.

WALKING THE DOGMATIC

Tell me, are you born again?
Are you aligned with a cause?
And is it cause enough to forget
your mother's birthday?
Do you live by rules or by drink alone?
Is smoking permitted in your house?
Do you have a healthy fear of the Lord?
Are you on a leash?
What is the name of your dogmatic?
Is your response automatic?
Do you stick to your guns?
Have you found the cost of your freedom?
Are you billed monthly, weekly,
or daily?

Have you lost your dogmatic?
Do you make your way alone, on a wing
or on a prayer?
Can anyone do anything in your house?
Is your house a house of prayer or
a den of contradictions?
Will you wear any color and vote
any which way,
depending on the weather?

You either got a cause or
you gotta pause.
You can eat, sleep and drink a cause
or eat, sleep and drink a pause.
You can believe in a pause or
believe in a cause.
You either wear it on your sleeve
or you're totally disarmed.
You either stick by your guns
or buy a ticket and watch

the arms race around you.
And then
when the arms race around you
you can cross your fingers
or count on a miracle.

34

IN BALI

The Balinese harvest two crops of rice a year.
Days before the rice is cut from the ground
they massage the roots and chant
soft repeating sounds.
They cut the rice with a special knife that
is concealed in the palm of the hand.
As if the rice had eyes.

In Bali
they dance and paint their faces.
The very old dance nearer to the demons
as they are closer to death
and the underworld.
And death itself is
one step closer to knowledge.

Everyone
returns to the village.
The shadow puppets dance splendidly.
Pig fat is offered to the demons.
A bony wrist measures the depth of water.
In Bali even the eyes are talented
and old men sport toothy grins.

BLOOD SISTER

Remember us sitting on the curb
on the left-hand side of the street
etching marks on flesh
pressing skin to skin?

Our blood freedom spilled down our wrists
and settled in a pool
like the afterthought
of so much background noise.

Our blood freedom stained kid skin
like the juice from a bruised grape
like wine loosening from beneath our tongues
the dribbled out oaths of
childhood promises

of faithfulness
of loyalty
of always togetherness —
ah! such sobriety!

EMANCIPATION SCREAM

Nights I just want to sit in front of a blank wall
  and scream.
Nights I just want to sit in front of a blank wall
  and scream.
Nights I just want to sit in front of a blank wall
  and scream.
Nights I just want to sit in front of a blank wall
Nights I just want to sit in front of a blank wall
  and scream

I wanna scream loud
I wanna scream louder and louder and louder and
  louder
and I wanna scream so loud
I wanna make the walls jump and the windowpane
  break all up
and down on the street I want the people to stop
cause I'm screaming so loud
they look up
scared shitless

I got my moments
you got 'em too
I just wanna
I just wanna
I just wanna be heard clear through to the other side
of this big old town
I wanna make a sound

I wanna
I wanna make
I wanna make a
I wanna make a
I wanna make a sound so
I wanna make a sound so

loud
so loud to make
uptown fall down

I wanna
I wanna crack open the flip side
I wanna turn the south side on its end
and the west end onto its east end and
I want the limos and the subways
I want them all to be
footpaths over a bridge into Brooklyn

I wanna scream
I wanna scream
I wanna scream loud
I wanna scream loud
I wanna scream loud enough
I wanna scream loud enough
to complete the highway
and to make the Statue of Liberty
a Statute of Emancipation.

I want the stationary to be an emotional line
I want the stationary to be an emotional line

I want the bums on the street
to be treated to meat and
I want the rich bitches to
beg for their pearls and
I want the big bosses
to give back the money and
I want the stationmaster
to turn the train around
I want the stationmaster
to turn the train around

I want the drug dealers to

sell roses and
I want the rose sellers to
do drugs till they drop down dead and
I want the bag ladies to
clean up their acts and
I want the actors to
stop driving hacks and
I want the cabbies to
speak my language

I want the east side to
go west young man and
I want the west side to
fall into the river and
I want the Statue of Liberty to
be a Statute of Emancipation

and finally
I want an explanation for the high cost of living

THOUGH SILENCE WAS YOUR INTENTION

The prediction
that the sun would shine and address
the issue of unkept promises
was an arrogant
mistake
now
the clouds hang
in a sky that threatens
and a less than subtle
measure of madness
reigns
now
against better judgment
I accept without debate
the wind's fury
that describes the rage
of gods
now
the full setting moon
and the dark days
and the immeasurable depth of water
and the tragedy of extinct species
are all beautiful

compared
to the silence
that was
your
intention.

I CONFESS

I confess my impatience!
The candlelight flickers,
the dawn's light advances, and
the chill in my bones describes
the terror that paralyzes
my proud mental powers.
Christ! I call upon you now!
I cannot wait for your second coming.
My sins are like live things
crawling in the pit of my belly,
as foul as the cockroaches swarming
in the cracks in my walls.
And I confess that my appetite
for death grows stronger
by the hour.

I confess my vanity!
I have seen with my two eyes
how devils spin webs
as cleverly
as spiders in corners.
And I beg you, yes you,
the very Christ that I,
in excess of nature,
betrayed with a thousand vile
intentions, receive me,
and make me now the object
of your divine intervention.
I fall on my knees and fold
my hands. I am practiced in all
things to the point of perfection.

Still, I confess my hunger!
Call a tree, a tree!
Call the earth, the earth!

But call upon me now
and I will believe
you are the very root
of all things.
And I do believe,
thief that I am,
that every leaf strives to God,
weeps to Christ,
and lives a sinless life.
Ah! But man is unlucky, no?
And seeks bread, by fair means or foul,
to satisfy his need.

I confess my ambition!
Christ! It is this last effort
of love which gives me energy.
It is my implicit trust in the
promise that grief passes quietly
into joy
that stays me.
I love you, and loving you,
I torment myself. And if I begged you
would you ready me
for sudden departure?
And if all men be servants or masters,
make me servant to the servant.
You see, there is still time to
prevent something terrible.

But, I confess my despair!
I am frightened beyond
the scope of my intelligence.
Console me with the promise
that all blood will be returned
to the sweet taste of wine.
Say it isn't true that we will end
by flooding the earth with blood

that cries out for more blood.
But, if I be fit only for slavery,
then satisfy, yes and even multiply
my desires. Truly I will go then
to my spiritual suicide.
It is my luxury. Poorer men than I
envy this drunkeness.

I confess my fear!
Christ! I call upon you!
Yes, I am angry about something,
and who can tell what?
I, in excited anticipation
can see nothing.
Is it not my place to look
into the soul? And will its
turn come?
I hold my breath, listening
and listening for someone to knock.
And I, who firmly resolved to sleep
without dreams,
beg in the final hour
some bargain be struck between us.

I confess my patricide!
It is true! I speak lies,
even here, and I demand lies,
even from you!
I weep for my father, as you cried
out to yours in that last hour,
Father, why hast thou forsaken me?

But who is the side
and who is the thorn?
Or are we both
each to the other? Yes, it is true,
every process has its law.

It is said, Science has as its object
all the senses and dismisses spirit
as if in triumph
over the senseless.

I confess my belief!
The candlelight is extinguished.
And, yes, in the midst of darkness
and every sin,
there is a glimmer, the
reminder of lightness and being.
And believe me,
I am not impatient for a miracle.
My faith suffers only a
simple thirst for justice.
I am carried away with my emotion;
I am moved by your silence.
But I confess
I do not know how to love
and I will end up
arriving at complete solitude.

ECLIPSE

I pulled my body through
the false opening in mama's belly.
The doctor lost his nerve and
didn't spank me.
Weighing less than a cornish hen,
I fought like a dog.
Two months later I was rewarded a proper bath
by my mother's father.
Liquid was fed to me through plastic.
I didn't have the words or nerve to ask
for mama's breast.
And papa might've killed me.
Yes, grace was promised me but
grace was denied.

I found solace staring
at the unchanging eye of the bulb above me.
I fixed my ears on sounds around me
but refused, like a monkey,
to tie into anything human
till I curled my infant fingers
around papa's bony wrist.
I still suck on the bittersweet memory
of mama's blood and guts around me.
My long fingers curl around the outline
of the October moon when it passes
between sun and earth.
I hold my breath and tread water
waiting for a proper birth.

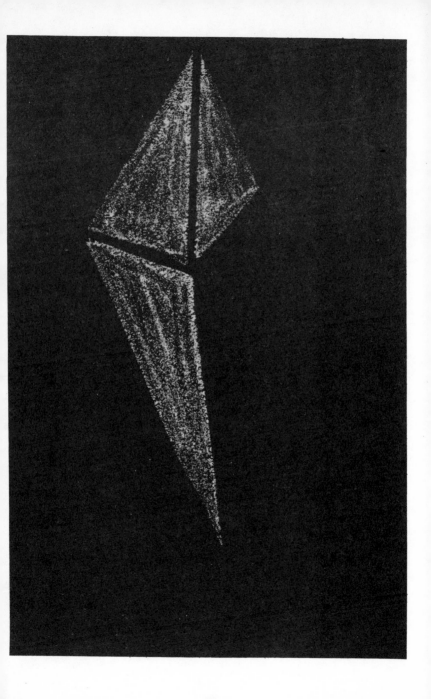

MARATHON

it's an empty book of matches
it's an open hand
it's a wound
it's an immigrant dream at a table
it's a hill of beans
and it's a big price to pay
for a little thing.

who will pay with everything
who will leave with nothing
who will say
enough of this
i've had enough of thievery

leave me to my planet
toss out the blueprint
toss back a cold drink
leave the back door open
but fasten tight the seatbelt
it's the law

the bell sounds
i'm searched and found carrying
contraband
so give me a billion dollars
i'll need a sanctioned gun in hand
on the street tonight

bite your tongue
bite the bullet
even michelangelo had words
with the pope
now they're scrubbing
his colors clean

it's the old game

a con that passes on like a baton
hand to hand
on and on
it's a marathon.

PICNIC

We're crazy about a bad habit
and we're still breathing.
And there's breathing down our necks
and we're hot.

Our bodies sing.
Our minds go limp.
The brain fever subsides.
We're like animals
about a bad habit.

We snort.
We stomp like horses
and bark like dogs.
We let out a running yelp!

Yelp!
Houses of dead eyes
watch us.
Red lights stop us, green lights
start us up again.

There is a fine warm sun
burning us.
Meanwhile, the young buck lies in the grass
and stares.

ONE PAIR OF SOCKS AND LOVE

I remember his eyes
clearly blinking back the tears.
We were sipping expensive beers.
It was cold outside
but hot in here, and a hundred bodies
quickened in from the storm.

He said it slowly, rolling
the glass in his hands.
His money was on the table
and his t-shirt was tight against
his chest.

"Sometimes the hand ain't
connected to the brain. It's
nothing to worry about.
Everybody gets stabbed in the
heart, it's no big deal,
get my drift?"

I rolled around in the snow,
got it down my neck. His
beard was white with it.
It fell fast, rising around our
feet.
I wanted to fall like a child
but caught myself bending my knees.

At the Dakota
I saw her face in the window
and walked back to see it again.
But then, when she saw me, she
backed away, and it was just snow
falling against a dark glass.
So we skipped off and bought more brandy.

A thousand tiny lights blinked,
like irridescent snow, in the trees.
Inside people were lunching expensively.
We were cold then, on the outside
looking in,
all the time laughing
and kicking back the bottle in our throats.

We looked for the horses but I guess
they're no good in this weather and
it finally made my nose feel like it
wasn't there. I might've worn two
pair of socks, if I was thinking, but
I wasn't so my imagination took over,
get my drift?

One time I got to climb a tree.
One time I jumped a fence. When
I looked at the ducks I wondered
if they were cold but I guessed not.
Then we saw a cardinal, a dash of
red against a falling white
sky.

In the car the heat was on
and the seat back, and we watched
the snow on the windshield melt
in pieces like bodies in a ballet.
And we sat like that till
the glass was clear.
I lost a glove and found it again.

I guess we talked about everything
in the middle of the park
but I can't remember a word of it.
Everyone wanted to sell us drugs
and it was funny at first,
if you get my drift.

On some days, like on this day,
a man covered with snow can sound
like any man. Words form
like snow on a beard, and then,
just slowly, the glass is made clear.
And be it beer or brandy, the inside
where the child hides, finds what it
seeks—
A heart, a brain, a hand and
courage to fall backwards in the snow.

BAREFOOT AND PREGNANT

In a gay bar in the east village
you confess that you're barefoot and pregnant.
It is almost laughable.
There are no doors on the bathroom stalls
so you keep an eye out
and I squat unsteadily and
relieve myself hurriedly.
It's unhealthy, I know, but
it's just beer, so why worry?
Andy, the bartender, is sociable tonight.
He speaks three words to us
and we're grateful.
He is wearing a stunning blue glove
on his left hand and a yellow one
on his right. He doesn't wear a watch.
My guess is that he tends bar all night.

We discuss everything, as usual,
and if only the clock would stop
we might finally touch base
and call it safe. But
wasn't the poetry fine?
Isn't his style flawless, his movement
and his thin charm something
to savor long after the words are done with
and the reading of his soul is over?
I noticed your hair pulled back
in a tiny ponytail
and I thought it
lovely.

And the excitement in your voice
matched the blood coursing through
my veins and the quick two-step
in my heart. We were

believing again in the possibility
of immortality.
It just might be the empty stage
awaits the duality of our untrained voices.
We are, each one of us,
barefoot and pregnant,
without wheels, so to speak,
and victims of our age.
Staying at home is the safe choice
or perhaps the easy exit out
from this maze of
endless possibility.

MY HABIT

My habit is noiseless.
My habit is the naked bride, sad,
with thin lips; inelegant perhaps,
but *honest*.

My habit is loyal.
My habit is calm, unthinking, and
like roses; excessive perhaps,
but *skillful*.

My habit is miracle.
My habit is a passionate blade, and
polished; blunt perhaps,
but *cutting*.

My habit is endurance.
My habit is a fenced in filly, and fitted
with blinders; childish perhaps,
but *flawless*.

My habit is crooked.
My habit is a snake, and
writhing and twisting; gutless perhaps,
but *confident*.

My habit is grave.
My habit is a cadaver, and
grinning forever; buried perhaps,
but *living*.

AN INTUITION

I got an intuition about you.
You tread water.
I got an intuition about you.
You don't panic.
Yes, I got an intuition about you.
You're a butterfly.
You're a helicopter.
You're a wavelength in the wind.
I got an intuition about you.
You're five fingers on one hand,
ten toes on two feet and
a strong combination of blood and bone.
I got an intuition says
you're a twentieth century fox.
I got an intuition says
you're a skeleton key to a pandora's box
stuffed with dynamite,
ready to explode.

THE WISDOM AND THE DIFFERENCE

(for Robert and Mame)

The night deals gently with him now
that his thousand fingers number ten
like any other man.
His lady brings him flowers
sown by her hands in the soil of this
cleansed new land.
He burned his old clothes and it
smelled worse than burning skin.
And with that he broke the back on the
history of his sin.
The day is kind to his face, his eyes
are clear, his moments freer than they
have ever been from the odor of poison.

He kisses her breasts, she moves his soul
to landscapes of sky and water. His belly
is tight, his muscles tuned, his new name
sounds good as it rolls off his tongue.
No longer a thief, not even a beggar,
he buys time and crosses off the days with pride.
The night deals gently with him now
that his thousand fingers number ten
like any other man.
His lady brings him flowers,
he takes them in his hands and with
each torn off petal
every flower ends "she loves me."

WET DREAMS

I am up on the roof
with every person I am
and the one I admire most
stands at the edge
quite apart from the crowded
middle

where the sun is hottest
as if there is only one
landscape that can save us
as if heat is the answer
as if the edge is as
cold as a razor

and I disengage myself
from the one voice
I most
listen to
there is the sound
of bongos

in the air mingling
with the traffic
that is always
steamrolling the pavement
on the avenue
five flights down

just over the edge
it is Saturday
it is springtime
everyone is
out from
under the rocks

hawking their wares
competing for currency
and intimations of immortality
the population is exploding
in the face of
the promise of summer

shares are advertised
for houses near water
half shares and quarter shares
and for the lucky few
their full share
of wet dreams

we all
meet on the roof to discuss
the possibility
of absenting ourselves
from the empty avenues
of august

one more vote is needed
to make a decision
but the one on the edge
is caught up in a dream
of flight into
the sun.

WAVE

I'm looking for that giant white wave
to dive into head first.
I'm waiting for the one wave to match my
strength and to win my clothes
off my skin.
I'm wanting real bad to get tossed about
and forced under your wetness.
I'm waiting for your white hungry curl
to turn me upside down
like a Baselitz painting
so all my color is just color
and all my lines are lines only
and my form is brand new again.

And I'm waiting for the sun's blind
holy power to shut out everything else
but that speck of dust in my eye.
My retina will take form
and I'll follow it to the edges of
both sides of my eyes
and it will never disappear,
it will never disappear
for I will find it again and again.

Above all that I want my lids to burn thin
and my skin to peel thick
and then, when I'm brown enough,
after I'm red enough,
I'll be brown enough to know what it feels like
to be brown enough to know what it feels like
to know what it feels like to be black skinned.

I'm waiting for that giant white wave
I'm waiting for that giant white wave
I'm waiting and I'm looking

I'm waiting and I'm wanting
that giant white wave
to dive into head first.
I'm waiting for the one white wave to match my
strength and to win my clothes
off my skin.
I'm wanting real bad to get tossed about
and forced under your wetness.
I'm waiting for your white hungry curl
to turn me upside down
like a Baselitz painting
so all my color is just color
and all my lines are lines only
and my form is brand new again.

And I'm waiting for the sun's blind
holy power to shut out everything else
but that speck of dust in my eye.
My retina will take form
and it will never disappear,
it will never disappear
for I will find it again and again.

Above all that I want my lids to burn thin
and my skin to peel thick
and then, when I'm brown enough,
after I'm red enough,
I'll be brown enough to know what it feels like
to be brown enough to know what it feels like,
I'll know what it feels like to be black skinned.

Just tell me,
go ahead and tell me how,
when you painted his eyes blue,
what it felt like when the paint dried,
what it felt like when the paint dried
and your brushes were brand new again,

after they were all new again.
Tell me how you painted his eyes blue
and what it felt like.

Is your talent enough?
Is your talent enough?
Is your talent enough,
your talent enough to carry you past blue
past blue into black
past blue into black
coal black
ivory black
into steel blue black
into zen black?

I wonder
is your passion enough to keep you there
where the great white wave
meets the big black hole of my stare.
And I wonder
and I wonder
and I wonder
and I wait in wonder
and I wonder
is your passion enough to keep you there
where the great white wave
meets the big black hole of my stare.
I wonder, is your passion enough?

There's black music coming out of your white eyes.
There's white lies coming out of your black magic.
There's black music coming out of your white eyes.
Black music coming out of your white eyes,
black music coming out of your white eyes,
white lies coming out of your black magic,
white lies coming out of your black magic,
and there's a wild stare.

And there's a wild stare.
And there's a wild stare.

I feel your wetness.
I know all about wet dreams.
I've been there
and even if I wasn't that lady on the street
I felt the heat burn a hole in my face so
wide my two eyes turned into
one, one
wild, wild stare.
And even if I wasn't that lady on the street
your moist open lips found me somewhere
between two buildings where
skeletons pose at night for cameras of the dead.

I'm looking for that giant white wave.
I'm looking for that giant white wave.
I'm looking for that giant white wave.

ON THE NOTION OF FOREVER
BEING FINALLY OVER

I climbed up to my roof, pen and paper in hand, to write three or more poems on the notion of forever being finally over. I started each poem with a capital F and thereafter every line was written smaller. It is true that heat rises. It is true that the air is thinner. The higher up you go the more you gasp for it. I light a cigarette anyway. How do I say forever is over and make it stick? Where do I go from here if I really believe that the edge of this roof doesn't lead like a stair to the sky and the stars? This edge descends quickly, very quickly to the street. I keep thinking I want to jump off this edge. I keep picturing my body falling and hitting the pavement. I can already imagine the screams from the pedestrians carrying their groceries. There is an outdoor cafe on the street below. It is enough that the air is thick with car exhaust and city dirt. Should I make their breakfasts more miserable by landing squarely in a plate of scrambled eggs? Or should I try to choreograph a clean dive into a cup of cappucino?
Forever is a hard idea to come by at all let alone let go of it. Forever keeps on sounding beautiful long after it has turned ugly and unpoetic. No. There is no justice, prosaic or poetic. I should have hung up the receiver before I let you spill the beans by saying very quietly, "It's too late for you to injure me...forever is over." I should have moved into a highrise long ago so I could imagine a much longer, much sweeter fall to earth. Never live over a cafe. Somehow it kills all flights of fancy. After all, there are the eggs to consider.

SONG OF NODS

Lying in bed
almost asleep
  not quite asleep
almost at ease
  not quite at ease
almost at peace
  not quite at peace

  you nod off to the land of nod
          off to the planet called nod
          off to the calm of nod.

Lying on the roof
almost cold
  not quite frozen
almost naked
  not quite clothed
almost drunk
  not quite sober

i nod off to the land of nod
      off to the planet called nod
      off to the calm of nod

you nod no!
no!
never never again!

i nod yes!
yes!
again and again!

we keep crossing paths in our sleep.

THAT PERFECTLY QUIET LOOK

In a living room, perfectly beige,
accented in lavender, my hunger
goes out of control and my anger
laces the conversation over champagne.

How can I tell you,
I am never ready for coffee? After all,
the moon always keeps me awake, and
tonight, especially in full control, it is
my master and I serve it out of breath.
Anxious to please my hosts, I am a perfect
guest,
choking on ice cream.

What I miss terribly
is that perfectly quiet look shared by
strangers at separate tables
in a dark room thick with smoke and promise.

YOUR
THIN SKIN

is pulled tight
as on a drum
beaten by hands in a distant land
to distract the demons
to attract the gods
to dance wildly and
chant loudly
in counterpoint
to convince
the rain to save
the crops
to feed the tribe
to keep alive
the tradition
of human sacrifice.

Your
thin skin
is pulled tight
over veins
across muscles
to package the
intricate goings on
behind the scenes
to curtain off
the theatrics and
the acrobatics
the pulsing and flexing
the pumping and
soft hum of the beating heart
that keeps alive the tradition
of human life.

Your

73

thin skin
is pulled tight
to shield the ego
to defend the image
to fight infection
and indescretion and
every armed enemy's
intervention. And
hiding in a man's body
a boy's confusion
tests the ice with the
weight of confession
that keeps alive
the tradition
of truth.

AN EXTRAVAGANCE

It certainly was an extravagance
to know you. Even
your lectures on the lives of
ants and bees,
their colonies of intricate
patterning and matriarchal indulgences,
felled me, partly because
I harbor a secret reverence
for dirt and honey.
Even your outdated conspiracy
to draft a final plan and
impose a pure ideology,
made me wince, true,
but still fall on my knees
and swear allegiance.

It certainly was an extravagance
to know you. Even
when you changed your mind daily
about the nature of love
and the existence of God.
Even when you confused the lines
drawn between art and life,
even then I could hang up the phone and
paint from experience.
When you detailed the inner sanctum
of my farshots and mocked my maniacal
measuring, I could not forget,
but did forgive,
that trespass on sacred ground.

It certainly was an extravagance
to know you. And
it was a pleasure to hold you
even when I suspected, and was often certain,

that I was embracing nothing but air and
its immeasurable mystery,
its endless vacancy intermingling with
the terribly sweet smell of roses and
the stench of open wounds.
Even when you, quite without emotion,
told me you met
with your very special jury and
all hands raised to condemn me, even then
I was as a child who has her candy stolen away
but believes tomorrow will be sweeter still
than today.

It certainly was an extravagance
to know you.

FOREVER

Forever
Never was my favorite game.
And
Even
If it was beautiful
Rolling off your tongue
A bell sounded somewhere
Back in my brain and
My heart was alerted.
Forever
Once
Was the temptation.
Forever
Once
Was the promise.
Forever
Is always broken
And spoken of too often.
Still
Forever
Might
Never have turned ugly
If it was never the bond between us
Now severed.
Now hanging.

OF SEASONS AND CENTURIES

There are some people like me
who wait for the longest day
of the year
and then miss it
and wait again for it
and miss it again.
It is the middle of March
and already the air
is lighter
the days imperceptively longer
and the evenings louder
on the avenue.

Is it too late for me
to become part of this
twentieth century?

I think the trees are
renewing their strength
except for the ones
that died.
And on Saturdays
men and women dig the earth
and plant new seeds.
There is a foolish abandon
at midnight
that signals the beginning
of a new day.
Sometimes I open a beer in the morning
just to break the routine.

So turn, turn, turn.
And turn again.

There are lengths of

chain link fence
that bar the wrong wrists
from wearing
bracelets of gold.
Already the children
have refined their graffiti
on the walls
in the schoolyard.
Already the young
have been seduced
into the old game.

This century is in its final chapter.
There are too many authors
I've never heard the names of.

The hunger will come.
It always starts
all over again.
The very water
is a danger to the species.
And the dirt
glows unhealthily
and feels sinfully uncommon
under my thumbnail.
Death in every form imaginable
is headlined,
is underlined and
is italicized.

So turn.
And turn and turn again.

The banks of the rivers
are littered
with tiny skeletons and
other remains

of
the living.
We should have beat
a path out of here
but the path beat us to it.
We might have rolled
with the punches, but
the punches rolled us first.

A flag is raised
by all our hands
as if we have won something.

I could have picked up
all the parts.
I could have pieced
them all together.
I might've spent a thousand nights
on my knees,
but a voice whispered,
"No, don't bother,
forever is over."
Well, young as I might be,
forever
was nothing new to me.

So turn, turn, turn.

Just yesterday
you sensed something
in my voice
and asked me
what it was
as if I could tell you.
It has just changed for the worse.
I won't do anything crazy
but

I sure
feel like it.
It's a dangerous game.

A jury of my peers
finds me guilty.
Well, I'll raise my glass too.

I confess my crimes.
My neck is readied for
the rope.
My accusor stands
to put his arms around me
for the thousandth time.
And for the thousandth time
I'm thinking about paint
and form and content.
A bare bulb attracts
moths in summer. I wonder
will it ever be warm again?

And turn, turn, and
turn again.

Everything is relative.
Everything is just
and justifiable.
Everything is an equation,
an equal sign
between
seemingly different numbers.
And the answer
to the riddle
is suspect
and open to interpretation.
Time moves slowly.

My fingers describe
a fist of anger that is
peculiar to this century.

There is a pressure
behind my eyes
that the TV
put there.
Still
we might survive the bombs,
the bricks and the sticks
and the names
we call each other.
We might duck the bullets
if our hearts bend
like our knees.

So turn.

I discover an unopened
bottle and
I drink it and
I light a fire and
read a news magazine
cover to cover.
Well,
what will tomorrow become
if not itself
over and over,
again
and again?

Will I embrace the
close of this century?
If it's all a joke, it's funny

And if it's not a joke

and not at all funny
I can still appreciate
the gesture
and the attempt
at humor.
But I wonder
whoever decided
that the first day of spring
should be
the coldest
day
of the year?

Well, turn, turn, and turn
again.

And
let us whisper sweet nothings
and count them as something beautiful
like children do.
And advertise your eyes
as if they were unmade beds
to fall into.
And fall on your knees
and pray
like figures of beauty do.
And take the animal for a walk
before you eat it.

Words can be censored
but not grunts
so grunt.

Is it Armegeddon?
Or is it the beginning
of another season
in a new century?

Spring forward!
Fall back! Step lightly!
Right left
left right
and
bang the
drum
slowly.

And turn.

WITNESS

On the stand
will you spill the beans about my blood,
describe readily its pulse
and its fluid ill-behaved trespass
through tunnels inside my skin,
quite beneath the visible muscle?

Will you confess without modesty
that the eyes I was born with
are deeply imbedded with daggers of light
and cleave the night boldly;
the clear clean liquid
unearthing danger?

Will you fix your arrow on my heart
and with a studied aim
snuff out the beat that defies gravity
and convulsions of lust;
pumping potions of love and fully opened
to distances?

And off the stand
won't you embrace my body,
catch my eye,
and with a decidedly soft touch
engage my heart
and join the caravan?

SUICIDE MISSIONARY

Up on the edge
the final prayer on my lips
is a whisper
asking forgiveness,
begging the moment's kindness
absolve my sins and
quickly extinguish the flame's
lick.

Too light for earth, I am
too much bone for sky, I have
too little love to parallel
too much lust. And
too much misery to form riddles.
Too many continuous folds of drunkeness
and a lost tongue and a forgotten language
moan.

Arranged perfectly, my plan is
flawless, my fatality is beautiful
as a thorn on a rose stem.
Above the skyline, bitten with decay and obscenity,
I, in uncaged slow motion,
address my obsession with flight.
I spread ten fingers wide,
work my hands hard like wings,
and fly.

ROBERT SMITHSON* IS A SKY PILOT

Up
In the sky
There is a drawing left by the
Tail of a plane
And it is abstract
And for once doesn't advertise
Suntan lotion.
I quite enjoy its
Mysterious white lines.
Looks like a circle gone
Off center,
An idea gone sweet
And sour
Leaving an aftertaste
As undefinable as
Chinese noodles.
Actually

It looks like a
Noodle
Cooked to perfection
Not limp
Not hard
But *al dente*.
Perhaps it is, after all,
A ploy to get me to buy
A *Ronzoni* product.
I prefer to think not.
It is just a pilot's dream
Writ large like a painter's dream
Flung wide
Like a poet's dream
Rhythmic and compelling,
Twisting and turning
In and in on itself.

The sky
Writing/drawing
Has blown a mile east
But it still
Holds its shape and
With my perspective
Now changed
I think
Smithson himself resurrected
Is piloting
His private plane
Outlining
A private joke, finally
Relieving the earth
Of
His private
Dream.

*Robert Smithson, a pioneer in earthwork art, died in an aircraft accident, in 1973. His last completed work was *Spiral Jetty* in The Great Salt Lake, Utah.

BETWEEN THE TABLECLOTH
AND YOUR SHADOW

And a dramatic bare bulb hangs
   from the ceiling
   and illuminates the gravest intentions
   you address at night
   to four walls and a door.

And the tablecloth, and a
   blue cut glass goblet, and the
   polished silverware,
   all despise your hunger
   but serve well your appetite.

And well hidden away in a closet
   is your fine philosophy
   in the form of ceramic figurines.
   Your tiny son sleeps, across the hall,
   in the shade of your shadow.

And a dramatic bare bulb swings.
   An arc of light
   illumes paintings of naked boys
   engaged in acts
   of sodomy.

And somewhere between the
   tablecloth and your shadow
   is hidden a scarred wrist
   and a
   very pronounced contradiction.

THE COWBOY LAUREATE

The great mad commander
dug the muzzle of a .45 into my neck
and whispered, *I love you.*
The only explanation is
boys like to play with guns.
Personally,
I like target practice. I was interested
in becoming a cowboy once.

In Nashville
I liked the way they spoke.
They carried guns in the backs of their trucks.
There was a certain honor there.
But my rifle is locked away in somebody's closet.
Even my mother spit
when the possibility of danger
was articulated.

Like children,
my songs move in and out
of favor.
I never minded
waking up
to that kind
of
noise.

RASKOLNIK

A certain confusion is perfected at night.
You cross over the border.
You are a victim of madness,
lucid madness
but you are not half mad
even.
You cross over the border
to pursue your destiny toward darkness.
You are a victim of
modern realism
and its amazing happenings.

Along the path of blood and crime
to power
statues stand guard to frisk you
and relieve you of your
honor.
It is useless.
You are a fact of life.
You embody the peculiar habit
of exceptional conflict.
Your dreams
are your exit out and
entrance into
something new.

You assume a conventionally
beautiful pose
as one who brings flowers
to his lover.
But
it never penetrates your thinking.
You transgress the law.
You wade through blood.
And your conscience

will not accuse you.
All is permitted
between the epic and
a slice of life.

THE DEATH OF GENET

Outside the window
a full moon sneaks
between the buildings
like a whore.
The little thief
quickly steals away
into cover
of darkness.

Under sentence of death
he was born and
abandoned by a world
stocked with volumes
of liberation mythology.
"Thus," he said, "I decisively
repudiated a world
that had repudiated me."

He never learned the name
of his father and
so he never knew if he
was a born or a made
outlaw.
He was self-confessed;
an artist with an appetite
for perversity.

"In a nation of thieves,"
he said,
he saw "no special act"
in being a thief.
The terrors of solitude
fed the self-invented
fantasies in a bizarre
hall of mirrors.

A short bald man
with a muscular body
died yesterday morning
in a small hotel room
in Paris. All of his
possessions fit into
one small suitcase.
The little thief is dead.

R.I.P.

(for Federico Garcia Lorca)

When you have died forever
& the mirror cannot return your eyes
When you have died forever
& the shadow cannot trail you
When you have died forever
& the taste in your mouth is forgotten
When you have died forever
& the rich adventure is a poor substitute
When you have died forever
& clocks everywhere are faceless
When you have died forever
& children cut fresh flowers
When you have died forever
& silence like snow melts slowly
When you have died forever
& the planet and seasons spin wildly
When you have died forever
& shapes cluster and nests are uncovered
When you have died forever
& the moon winks and the black horse sleeps
When you have died forever
& every continent is a ship in danger
When you have died forever
& bitter tears injure the legend
When you have died forever
& every lost treasure is recovered
When you have died forever
& fingers beat the skin on a drum and
    sound low moans like branches in winter
When you have died forever
& all parted paths return you
    to five points on a brilliant star

rest in peace.

BROKEN PALISADES

Until we are immortal,
continuous with all things silenced,
set free from chance
and the tyranny of secondary things,
darkness reigns.

In a moment broken from
the circle of a dream
the fire of the world takes hold
lifting in the wind
all that burns behind me.
And,
after a long reeking silence,
my head rushes the clay walls of a city
that would muffle
the adventures of earth!

Whole bodies of gold glitter!
Bits of ships and shadows
urge silence to listen at my chest
to the fragile beat of a wild thing
seized with laughter!

Just one human word!
And the miserable shadows burst
back into flame.
Just one sound!
And she leaps, lashing her
unequaled tongues across our sobs;
divining beasts
to scheme
a greater galaxy of dust!

ASH OF THE OAK
(for Walt Whitman)

Bellying In The Wood, *the storm*

The quick thrill of the sharp snap of the tree is
    as potent as a sudden command to striptease
    for drunken men.
The crowd is riotous. All loot and plunder.
But I am rooted like a mighty oak and cannot
    surge forward or shrink back.
I remain poised for action as the shadow of myself
    leans dizzyingly out the window.

The grass beaten flat is less attractive than it
    is uncompromising.
Reality is a magic carpet ride threaded through
    the eye of unsilenced ambition.
Unashamed, I take certain pride in my schemes as I
    would in the perfect recollection of a dream.
But death is always, in some form, attractive.
Moths are forever drawn to light.
Immortality is treasured, but life is measured
    by patience for detail.
I, however, scratch at the door opening onto
    an attitude of power.

In a raging storm I am freed from the sages and
    unconvinced of mortality.
Lightning quickens my pulse, thickens my blood
    and excites a hunger that mocks my belly of despair.
Wind repairs these thin arms; my heart pumps the
    enraged blood of a mad crowd's rising appetite
    for scandal.
Caught in the eye of a thundering sky, exiled
    from the sun,
I rejoice that this noise is candidate for my affection.

Architecture's ambition is swiftly rendered artless
    and aimless.
And still I have an itch to emulate the master's stroke.

Every appearance is a show of strength.
My words quickly exhaust themselves when the reserve
    of unspent addiction chatters like teeth.
Proudly I flash my poverty and readily I enter
    into debate with the man in the moon.
I hold him in high esteem for I have re-enacted
    the crucifixion of the evening star and witnessed
    its five brilliant points driven through
    with flawless precision.
The rain on the mountaintop is constant as is
    a rainbow colored the mean hue of spent life.

Battle Cry Of The Wooden Soldier, *pinnochio's wood*

I, in my thirties, am older than most accomplished
    geniuses.
I kneel and repeat the rosary.
I am equal to these tongues of despair.
I am as playful as a spray of wild flowers,
    as graceful as a spotted fawn.
Time, however, is adamant, and penetrates the
    landscape.
The ghost of Pinnochio nods a greeting of
    recognition.
I reveal myself to him as a bead on a strung neck.
And I am unconvinced, at last, that limitless vision
    is the intuition of a butterfly.
It simply obeys an invisible law.
The tormented soul of man wins him the vital
    and devoted strength of woman.
And from between four thighs is sprung a
    caterpillar.

The wood suddenly springs to life like Pinnochio's
nose, and something fleshlike peeks out
from beneath the bark.
I re-enact the games of children.
I am a forager in the forest, I prey on
the innocent.
I am a voyager and the wood floats me home
in time to catch apprentices laying bricks
around the hearth.
I am tricked into throwing sticks on the fire.
A big bad wolf grins beneath the covers.
Pinnochio weeps in a corner.
Who carved so skillfully the flawless nipples
on his breast?
And who denied his wooden limbs and thick sweet
trunk a dropleaf between his legs?
Poor boy can't get it on or up and has to lie
again and again just to swell like a man...
Ah, Pinnochio! That nose!
Even a queen would bow down and lie with you.
And children smother you with wet kisses.

I steer my ship into deeper waters.
I am indifferent to beautiful faces that promise
the luxury of silken sheets and calm waters.
I weave a tapestry wholly unfamiliar with,
and baffled by, worms at work.
According to the planet, and to Michelangelo's
blueprints, buttocks can be pronounced
but the holy chamber is forever sealed
from the sight of half open eyes.
Shooting stars continue to defeat the sensible.
And caught between the wood is the concept of forever,
mistakenly caged.
Still I am overjoyed as I traverse the roofs.
I grow an army of limbs to defeat the impending tragedy.

Stays Against The Tide, *driftwood*

My commanding officer is the constructor of stays
    against the tide,
    the instructor that half closes my eye.
My creator cashes in on original sin and
    finds out the cracks in my alibi.
I am not surprised that my knees are not innocent.
I tunnel in the dirt like a common spider and
    seek revenge on the ax that threatens to fell me.
Unashamed, I count on and covet the adventures
    of the flesh.

Would you question my pride, you who shaped
    my firm desire to be larger than life?
It is enough that I am possessed by your breath,
    shaped by your hands, envisioned by your eyes.
In your image I roam the earth, wielding a singular
    match to burn my bridges with.
I plunder the gaps but refuse to grovel in this dirt
    or bargain for yet another hour of sun.
Haven't I begged your pardon daily?
And daily prepared a simple supper?
My contempt for statues and ceremony does not change
    the fact that paint is peeling off of a rotting canvas
    that begs restoration.

My exclusive right remains that death be exhilerating,
    and you, my dear secreted friend, must not deny one
    who has feasted on blood and flesh.
The thirsty must not be denied a cupful of wine, nor the
    hungry, bread.
My unholy appetite, wedded to my tongue-in-cheek
    irreverence, is swiftly defeated by nature's rage.
I have long hidden between the pages of dead authors,
    the easy prey of dead men and women.

I hurry to the sea but I am like an island whose beauty
and meaning have been maligned by tired souls
trespassing the landscape of belief.
I return again and again to the gash of winter, the dash
of autumn's brilliant color, and the strong, strange
scent of spring.
Summer, as distant as the daughters of my father's
sister, is as alluring as my blood brothers.
The city dulls my senses after having cut off my beak
of vision and saps my energy.
But with a reserve of strength I chew on salt
and swim the laps of indifference.

Some say burial is barbaric, yet somewhere in the back
of the mind is harbored a desire to enter into the
earth's mysterious center.
Why then, am I so adamant that my ashes be scattered
at sea and insist on the accompaniment of a blues
band to issue forth tunes from Broadway?
The invitation has gone out, and be advised,
crashers are welcome.

My final plea ends up lodged between my heart and
tongue, and like a cat I claw a carpet that
has lost its magic.

Parting In The Wood, *timber!*

I awake from my dream to find the mast intact.
Shapes rise around me.
Even the pyramids cannot compare to the industry
of my hands.
I mold a fair likeness that insinuates God is
a useful invention.
Still, I insist on bread and wine and cross myself

countless times.
Forgive me.
Mine is simply an artful stance.

And can't you guess?
I loved you so much that I could not help hating you too.
I loved you so much that I address the space you filled
   when you faced me with your manhood intact
   and your eyes just open.
I loved you so much that my womanhood split into
   factions to accommodate you.
And each faction, with unparalleled adoration,
   served you.
My mother instinct spoonfed your hunger,
   my lady-in-waiting smile engaged your whims,
   my queen's airs mocked your simply adequate limbs,
   my painted eyes and swollen mouth devoured
      your lust,
   my girlish fancies lured your boyish schemes to
      completion,
   but my goddess instinct leveled your king's ambition.
No.
Ours was no missionary position...

Even now, as I practice my widowhood,
   you bury your head between my thighs and bawl
   like a monkey.
My adult affectations melt like a forged gold shilling.
Prepare to be stunned
         Rapunzil finally lets down her golden hair.

VICE AND VIRTUE

I drink!
I drink to excess!
I drink
till I fight it
to stay awake
hardly alive.

I smoke too many
brown tipped cigarettes
and I wait for the prognosis
to be bad
for the test
to prove positive.

And when I love you
it's like I drink you
and when I love you
it's like I smoke you up
till I'm gasping
for air.

When I love you
the way I love you
it's like I'm waiting for you to kill me.
Then I'll stop drinking
and stop smoking
and loving you.

   After
I can't open my mouth on you and
   After
I can't suck you and
   After
I can't feel your breath in my ear

Then
we'll stop breathing
Then
when we stop drinking
Then we'll be dead
in the arms of each other.

Till we die like that
I'll drink to excess and
I'll smoke
and I'll love you till
the test proves positive
and the air too thin to whisper

I love you.

TWO HUNDRED
MEANINGFUL SEXUAL RELATIONSHIPS

He was not at all an old man, and he was attractive enough, but a bit of a braggart. I heard him say, from the far end of the bar, that he has had over two hundred meaningful sexual relationships. I put my beer down when I heard that! Already I was counting on my fingers, and it floored me that my two hands were one too many to even make a stab at competition. Then I tried to think of two hundred meaningful glances that might've passed for intimacy of a kind, and I couldn't get past my ten fingers and the five toes on my left foot. I finished my beer quickly and ordered something stronger. A man next to me said, "Looks like it's gonna be a long night. Got a lot of catching up to do, hey?" He was on his fifth bourbon and I couldn't help but admire his perspective on things. I said that to catch up would require a cast of a hundred on my part. He mentioned that he had two cats and a dog. I caught on and laughed. "Yeah, after all, dog is man's best friend."

Well, needless to say, I went home alone and watched *Casablanca* for the twenty-seventh time. After all, I have a certain reverence for numbers too.

THE UNENTITLED

You are just like me,
dedicating everything that you haven't done
to everyone you have ever loved.
You are just like me,
polishing the title before the content
has been decided.
And more and more like me,
you have stars in your eyes
and imagine immortality
and the rising applause
congratulating the outfit
you have chosen with care
for the night of the big performance.

Just like me,
you breathe deep, drink hard,
curse fate and all the gods.
Our untrained voices,
in a unison that is flawless,
praise the little thief
who finally escaped with all his jewels
hidden in a tiny suitcase.

But a lifetime cannot be measured
by titles and dedications,
and all the sequined and tailored outfits
cannot clothe or make invisible
the blood jumping in our veins.
Like wretched junkies we seek a fix
to dull our pain
and compensate for our lack of title
and our too constant dedication
to everyone we have ever loved.

TIED UP, FATTENED UP, EATEN UP
(*night of the iguana,* revisited)

Somehow, somewhere,
when your hands and belly are
empty and
both eyes are half open and
the sky is threaded with clouds
and the sun
is uncertain
how to loose night
upon the planet,
the spook'll get ya.

Yes, the spook'll get ya,
somehow, somewhere,
when miles from your nest
sorrow triumphs and tears fall,
when traps set
snare the sacred moment poised
between day and night, and
one dream crosses into another
and the love between singer and silence
is unveiled.

Somewhere and somehow,
when the measure of life is weightless
and abandoned by history,
when you spy on children and
the sounds of the carousel ring in
your ears and
the breach of trust is caused
not by lust
but by innocence shaken and compromised,
the spook'll get ya.

Yes, the spook will get you,

somehow and somewhere
where love is either madness or artless.
And when you have unlearned your
liberty and
you have returned to the place
called home and
find that the monster is in you,
realize full well,
the spook awaits you.

SCENES

Always on stage
    he speaks loudly in bars
    of perversity
    and insists
    talent for madness
    is cause for
    applause
    and encore.

The actor
    controlled by a script
    insists
    a degree of drama
    is no more terrible
    than
    a degree of
    freedom.

And a forged chain
    as cold as pain
    confuses
    law and every
    act of love
    with
    truth and
    honesty.

Embedded
    in the past, and
    locked by fate
    into
    a fired performance
    the actor's grasp on life
    belongs
    to somebody else.

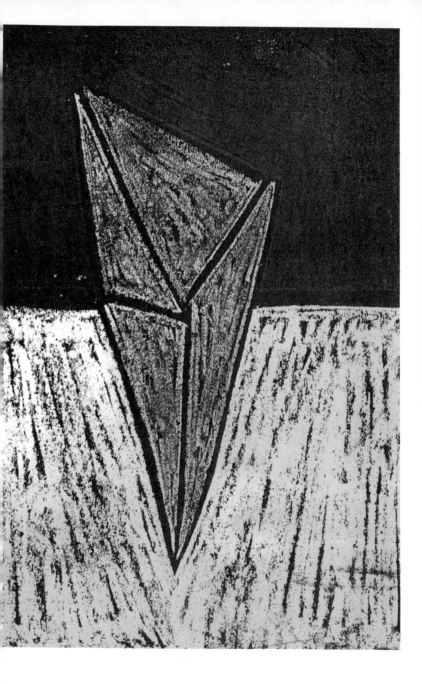

A NORMAL CONVERSATION

how's your life
how's your life?
   your sex life
   your work life
   your wife life?
how's your job, huh
hey, how's your job?

LOVE IT LOVE IT I LOVE IT!

are you ever depressed
are you ever depressed?

NEVER EVER EVER DOWN ever sad?
NO NOT EVER EVER SAD!

hey how's your GREAT FINE
hey how's your GREAT FINE

   I'M COMPLETELY DETATCHED

hey how's your COMPLETELY DETATCHED
   COMPLETELY UNCONNECTED
   GREAT FINE
   UNCONNECTED
   UNINJECTED
   UNINSPIRED
   COMPLETELY DETATCHED
   I LOVE LIFE FROM ALL SIDES
   I LOVE LIFE FROM ALL SIDES
   I LOVE LIFE FROM ALL SIDES
   I'M COMPLETELY DETATCHED
   I'M COMPLETELY DETATCHED

do you ever drink to escape

do you ever drink to escape

        I NEVER DRINK AT ALL

        I DON'T TOUCH THE STUFF

NOT EVER EVEN EVER TOUCH THE STUFF

are you happy YES

are you happy YES

are you happy I'M COMPLETELY DETATCHED

are you happy COMPLETELY DISCONNECTED

COMPLETELY COMPLETELY COMPLETELY

I WANNA SPEND MY LIFE WATCHING TV
  AND DRINKING BEER
I WANNA SPEND MY LIFE WATCHING TV
  AND DRINKING BEER

      OH I'M SORRY I SAID THAT
      i'm sorry you said that
      I'LL NEVER SAY IT AGAIN
      i'm sorry you committed a sin
      I'LL NEVER DO IT AGAIN
      I'M SORRY I COMMITTED A SIN
      I'LL NEVER DO IT AGAIN

      I'M NORMAL   I'M NORMAL

completely without a doubt NO DOUBT ABOUT IT
no question about it   I'M NORMAL
     COMPLETELY ALTOGETHER FULLY
without a doubt no doubt about it
NO QUESTION ABOUT IT I'M NORMAL
HEY

      I GOT POISE
      I'VE SEEN THE WORLD
      I'M COMPLETELY NORMAL

```
            I GOT POISE
            I'VE SEEN THE WORLD
            I'M COMPLETELY NORMAL

     I'M UNINHIBITED WITHOUT HANGUPS
            I ENJOY QUIET DINNERS
     I'M UNINHIBITED MINUS HANGUPS
            I ENJOY QUIET DINNERS

     I WANT TO SPEND MY LIFE WATCHING TV
            AND DRINKING BEERS
     I WANT TO SPEND MY LIFE WATCHING TV
            AND DRINKING BEERS
                    I'M SORRY I SAID THAT
                    I'LL NEVER SAY IT AGAIN
                    I'M SORRY I COMMITTED A SIN
                    I'LL NEVER DO IT AGAIN

do you ever wonder
I NEVER WONDER
why
WHY I NEVER
do you ever wonder why
I NEVER WONDER WHY
               I'M COMPLETELY DETATCHED
                    COMPLETELY  UNCONNECTED
               I'M COMPLETELY UNCONNECTED
do you ever NO I NEVER
did you ever NOT EVER
would you ever NO I NEVER

            ever?    NEVER!
```

THE WORM MOON

Is there no constellation
called Worm?
What can I do but
connect the stars differently
and redefine centuries of saga?
I'm arrested by this moon.
I imagine my delicate skin
leaves fleshprints in the dirt
as I, summoned forth by spring
slither out from under
my winter rock.

What joy now!
To feel the sun's heat on my face
and to be up here again on my roof!
It is the Worm Moon
and I am the worm, out from
underneath my skin, lying on
my belly in the wind,
clipping off the edge of
winter's chill.
What joy now! To be naked and brand new,
my thousand legs readied to run!

Somewhere there must be a flower ·
without name.
Somewhere exists a gate
with entrance into song and celebration.
Driven by nature's harp, I confess
a dream I have —
Across my garden, and
beyond its wall,
are innocent lambs unslaughtered,
rocks yet unturned.

It is the Worm Moon and

I am a worm.
Daylight welcomes me into
her merciful embrace.
It is the Worm Moon and I am a worm.
I exhale months of worry.
I inhale the hot taste of summer
and connect the dots differently
to fashion a map
scaled to my dreams.

LETTER TO A FRIEND OR TWO

I can trust you not to kill me, right?
I have to have someone
to trust not to kill me
so would you be that someone?
    Let me scream at you!
    You can scream at me.
    Let me cry out next to you!
    I'll cry with you.

Let me be cool around you.
Let me be a fool around you.
Let me put my arms around you.
Let me open my mouth on you.
Let me let you take me between the legs
if you want to.
If I want to.
    Don't worry, really, don't worry.
    We won't do it
    but I'd let you, I'd really let you,
    if you wanted to, I'd let you.

I like the way your voice sounds
on the phone.
I like the way the sound comes
in your throat.
I'd like to market a bottle of your breath.
I guess the only thing is
I won't let you kill me.
And I promise
I won't kill you or even make you die
a little.

Look, honesty *is* important
and it *is* the right straight way to fly
and all of that

but I don't know,
it just seems to me that sometimes
honesty spoils all the fun we're having
pretending.
You know, I never understood,
except vaguely, the difference
between a *mortal* sin and a *venial* sin.
I remember one was a lot darker than the other.
   There were times I saw my soul
   like it was some big black hole —
   nothing good going into it,
   nothing good coming out of it.

Truth is a drug.
It's a hard drug.
You'll go on to harder drugs
and if you try to stop telling the truth
it'll hurt you real bad.
You'll hurt so bad you'll wish you were dead
but you don't die.
But take it from me, *it'll kill you.*

Hey, don't thank me.
I won't thank you, we don't have to
so let's not.
I'd thank a stranger on the street
but I know you too well for that.
And you know what?
You can even pretend to be you
when you're with me.
It's just like having fun on monkey bars.
It's just like when we catch each other's eye
in the middle of anywhere.
It's just like a wink.
   Words aren't necessary
   except maybe to say
   they aren't necessary.

Call me up on any day of the weekend
and I'll play catch-22 with you.
Let's play hot potato too
and let's pull out the crayons, the *toxic* ones.
Let's take drugs together.
Let's play ball.

THE TOY BOX

You break off every breath you inhale,
Exhume every body you impale with that
Devastating luxury of style.
One question remains:
Would you kill or be killed?
Would you arm your naked boy with
A gun, and hope he finds the trigger
To test his strength
Against the army of indifference?
Would you thrust him barelegged,
Chest open for the arrow?
I wonder that his hand touching grass
For the first time didn't make you
Beg another saviour onto earth,
Sprung from a distant land and
An undocumented religion.

All those masters of the universe
Strewn on childrens' floors
Are the newest false idols.
Would that they could fashion
A globe, from this, our tiny map.
Would that they, with their glorious
Talents, could sever the distance
Between planet earth and each star.
Would that those giant ideas
Could trample every flag and
Proudly haul up one banner
That our childrens' eyes might
Pledge allegiance to.

Offer your son, instead of a gun,
A wholly rewritten bible
And place that tiny hand on
To swear in a first just law.

All those masters of the universe
Jammed inside the toy box
Are the newest false idols.
Where did you go, G.I. Joe?
A nation turns its lonely eyes to you.

TWENTIETH CENTURY PATRIOT

Like a true American
I believe in everything and in nothing.
I left church, palms in hand
and hailed a cab uptown.
In five minutes my faith was near
collapse and I was
ready to embrace the law of Islam.

I am afraid to swallow medicine,
certain it will kill me.
I love my fellow man but admit fear
when late at night
footsteps sound behind me.
My honesty gets me into deep water
and my arms and legs fail me.

I am an exile from domesticity
yet I dress my mantle with
flowers arranged aesthetically.
I beg some one thing to merit
the attention of my eyes
for five minutes longer than
my belief in God lasted yesterday.

Everyone's politics are okay by me.
Every flag is raised by me.
Every master is served by me.
Every race is embraced by me.
All crime is forgiven by me.
All lust is sanctioned by me.
Every border is crossed by me.

I am every man and every woman.
I am every animal desire.
I conspire against every idea

ever proven to me.
I am a true American.
I believe in everything and
in nothing.

I SHOULD NOT HAVE

I should not have walked so bravely
Through those streets, nor
Held so very tightly the grey in his hair.
I should have offered my body to
A thousand men before him, and
Made them all relatives of a kind.
I should never have tested the ice
With my full weight, nor let my
Teachers clothe my naked body with
Their inventions.

I should not have thought
Each day a private gift from above.

I should not have scored his initials in
My arm, had I known how easy it is
To change a name.
I should have numbered the days
With the fine mathematics of the Arabs
Had I known there is no infinity
Save in the sand. Even the bottom of
The ocean is a hard place and the
Planets have their limits.
I should have gloved my hand
Before I discovered my nails
So I should never have torn out
My heart.

I might weep but for my eyes that
Are frozen open on the old calendar.
Still, I would not cheat, even now,
A king's son out of a taste of this,
My very cold body. My dark soul.

A BED OF FEATHERS

He said,
"You threw too many feathers at me
till one found its mark
and like a bullet felled me."

I said,
"I was only trying to soften the blow,
and make a bed for you
to lie in."

IT MUST BE LOVE

He said not to worry
when the hand is not connected to the heart,
but worry I do.
I turn up the music and
pop open a bottle of champagne.
Some kind of worry is this.

The fire burns bright and
I think of tigers in the night,
this the year of.
Across the street a policeman stands,
his hand on his gun.
Already I feel stronger.

And you would not believe
how I laugh
after I paint my heart out;
another St. Valentine's Day massacre.
I have, I guess,
a peculiar sense of humor.

Tonight it would be fine
to have company up here in my rooms.
The 'ol bubbly is working a heat
through me, and if I could control
my laughter and my eyes,
no one would be the wiser.

Perhaps an old movie will do the trick,
or a walk in the snow, yeah, down the hall,
four flights below.
Lord knows there's action of every kind
and a thousand hands
unconnected to the heart.

And,
I think of angels and saints and ashes
in the form of a cross smudged on your forehead.
You looked like a walking Jesus.
I didn't mean to laugh.
I was in a devilish mood.

It must be love makes me
make the bed up and open it again each night.
It must be love lets me let you
babble on about Presidents and Kings.
It must be love. But Lord!
What a mystery life is late at night.

WHEN THINGS GO VERY BAD

I was taught a long time ago
by a man with shoulder length blonde hair
and an earring
to take a blade of grass and
knot it three times.
"Then hold it behind your back,"
he said,
"and when night descends,
toss it."
He said, without trace of humor,
without irony or hint of ridicule,
"this will ward off the demons
and keep you safe till morning comes."
I was young then.
I asked, "What happens
when the night is over
and the dawn comes? Won't all those
demons reappear as if summoned
by the smell of coffee brewing?"
The man with the shoulder length blonde hair
and an earring
said to me, without trace of contempt,
without guile or derision,
"Didn't Christ rise upon the third day?"

Naturally
none of it made sense to me.
I persisted. I asked if he
might teach me a chant,
"something to reverse the situation
when things go very bad."
He said,
"You are very young, aren't you?"

Well, years have since taken their toll.

I have developed a wrinkle
over my left eye and I am warned
that my reverence for sun
will age me considerably
and finally kill me.
The man had his hair cut off
and his earring hole is healed over.
His speech, I am told,
is thick with sarcasm, irony and
contempt.
I am all alone
with my little wrinkle and
my appetite for heat.
My rooms are littered with blades
of grass, thrice knotted.
Paintings of the crucifixion hang
on my walls.
I attend Easter services.
Still I search rare books for something to
chant aloud
now that the nights seem unending
and the day's light
unexpectedly stays away.

THE FACE OF A MAN JUST OFF THE CROSS

For once I want to see
and if only once
the face of a man just off the cross
a face still bearing traces of warmth
and life
a face still bearing the detail
of infinite agony
yes
and if only once
the face of a man wounded
tortured and beaten
and crucified six hours
a face crushed by blows
actual blows
eyes swollen and bruised
half open
not symbolical
but actual.

THE GOOD PROVIDER

The good provider stalks angrily.
The sun sets early in the fall
and we are left with
too many hours of
darkness.

Danger is more apparent.
We are grossly confused.
The doors are locked.
The gun is cocked.
The barrel is aimed at our throats.

My camera is jammed.
Gridlock is common.
The phone is ringing.
I pick up the receiver.
It is dead.

APPLES AND ORANGES

The vast landscape between
thought and action
is the very particular distance
between
armchair love
and lust.
And even a firm faith in
immortality
cannot save a poet
felled by an act
of terror.
But that flowers bloom at all
is enough
for the poet
to stare down the barrel of a gun
and dispute the bullet
that silences the heart
and its fluid instinct.

NOT AN OLD STORY

Never say die!
Never say die!
Exchange crosses or anything else
you hold sacred.
Blood, if you like.
The fact is that
there are no old stories.
The fact that I was born
is not an old story.
The fact that I will die
is not an old story.
Five fingers on my left hand
is not an old story.
Ten toes, two feet, a mouth and a nose,
two eyes, two ears, thumbnails and
elbows and wrists and hair follicles
are not an old story.
Muscle spasms, heart attacks, heat strokes,
cut veins, cat scratches and
empty books of matches
are not at all an old story.
High rises, teepees, mud shacks,
mole holes, caves of bats and
gutters of rats
are not an old story.
Nothing is an old story.
Everything deserves its moment of birth.
That I am alive at all
is not an old story.
That I awake from a dream
is not an old story.
Never say die!
Never say die!
Exchange crosses or anything else
you hold sacred.

Yes,
blood, if you like!

THE CHOICE

If you smile, life makes you laugh!
If you cry, you are consumed by death.
If you purse your lips
the fine line exists
and you can tightrope walk it to the end,
but no one will know what you're thinking.